THE HARVEST OF LESSER BURDENS

ART IN THE FIELDS OF MEDICINE

A collection of poems, paintings, and photographs
from the 1998-2003 Artists In Residence Program
at the Washoe Medical Center in Reno, Nevada

THE HARVEST OF LESSER BURDENS

ART IN THE FIELDS OF MEDICINE

This book is set in Minion Pro and News Gothic Std.

Library of Congress Control Number: 2006926531
ISBN-10: 0-9764800-2-6
ISBN-13: 978-0-9764800-2-0

Designer: Shelly Bohach, Nevada Museum of Art
Printer: A. Carlisle & Company, Reno, Nevada

Image (front cover):
Sharon Maczko, *Steps Toward Recovery*, 1999, transparent
watercolor, 36" x 25.75", from the *Washoe Medical Series*.

Epigraph (front cover):
Hayden Carruth. "Donald Hall's House of Virtue Built in the
Woods and Fields of Time," *The Day I Was Older, On the Poetry
of Donald Hall*, edited by Liam Rector. Story Line Press, 1989.
Page 70. Reprinted with permission from the author.

Shaun T. Griffin. "The Heart Donor," *New Century North
American Poets*, edited by John Garmon, Donna Biffar and
Wayne Lanter. River King Poetry Press, 2002. Pages 163-164.
Reprinted with permission from the author.

CONTENTS

FOREWORD

In 1997, Washoe Health System (WHS), now Washoe Medical Center, and the Nevada Museum of Art partnered on the Healing Arts Festival, an exhibition of art on the theme of "Art That Heals," organized tirelessly by John Tresise of the WMC staff. Through this festival I had come to know Darleen Luster, behavioral health and Healing Arts Festival coordinator for WMC, and we were interested in exploring other ways in which the hospital and museum could collaborate. A few months later we met for lunch, and Darleen shared a conversation she had just had with a patient. This particular patient, a competitive athlete and mountain-biker, had recently been in an accident while riding his bike. Darleen had to break the news to this patient that his accident had paralyzed him from the neck down.

On hearing this story I was moved not only by the tragedy of this individual patient, but also in the realization that this is a story that replays itself day after day within the hospital environment. Every day hospital staff balances the emotional chaos of tragic and sad stories with the wonderful stories of recovery. Our conversation on collaboration became more pointed as we began to think about these stories, the daily stories of the hospital experience, and how they could be translated to the greater community.

The hospital environment is a particularly intense atmosphere where life and death decisions and the repercussions of those decisions occur daily. Unless one has had an intimate experience within a hospital, it may be difficult to fully comprehend the grave reality these patients and caregivers experience daily. It was in these preliminary discussions that we began to explore ways in which artists could provide a unique and poignant interpretation of this environment. We decided on a residency program where selected artists would become, in essence, hospital employees. For this to work, the artists needed wide-ranging access to the departments and specialties within the hospital, an access practically unprecedented in the hospital community. We, in turn, needed full support from the hospital administration and staff for this program to be implemented.

In a series of meetings, Darleen and I introduced the concept to Lynn Atcheson (then vice-president for communications for WMC) and Jan Johnson (Washoe Medical Foundation director) and received positive support for the idea. Jan Johnson enthusiastically became the coordinator of the program pledging foundation funds as well as raising additional grant funds to help support the residencies.

From the beginning of an idea to an approved concept, we next had to develop a process. We decided that we would select three artists for residencies in 1998-2003. The artist selection committee was composed of Reno artist and scholar Jim McCormick, Jan Johnson of WMC, and me. We looked for artists who worked in different media who we believed could work effectively within a hospital environment. We quickly settled on Sharon Maczko, a watercolorist of exceptional skill; Stephen Davis, a documentary photographer whose images are intricately connected to text and stories; and Shaun Griffin, a respected poet with a remarkable sense of observation and compassion. All three artists graciously agreed to participate in the program as well as go through an orientation training to introduce them to the hospital environment. Each was allowed, over time, access to whatever program intrigued them: Sharon spent her time in neurology; Stephen in oncology; and Shaun primarily in pediatrics.

Once the artists were selected, Jan Johnson took over the reins of the program. She shepherded each artist through the hospital's orientation process, made certain that the artist interactions within the hospital environment were understood and accepted by hospital staff, and acted as an advisor and confidante to each of the artists during and following their residencies. The "Artist in the Hospital" program could not have occurred without Jan's commitment and passion for the program.

These artist residencies were unique and challenging for the artists and the hospital community. But the goal of the program was to convey what the artists learned to the non-hospital community, to somehow represent to the general public the nature of the hospital experience from the patient and staff perspective. I am pleased and proud that the Nevada Museum of Art and Washoe Medical

Center have joined together, once again, to publish this book, *The Harvest of Lesser Burdens: Art in the Fields of Medicine,* as the complete documentation of this residency experiment and to make it available to all in our community.

On behalf of the Nevada Museum of Art, I want to thank the artists, Sharon Maczko, Stephen Davis, and Shaun Griffin, for their commitment to this concept and impassioned response to their residencies. I also want to thank Washoe Medical Center, its administration, staff, and patients, for opening its doors and hearts to this project and allowing the artists to have unfettered access to the Center's work and thoughts. The Washoe Medical Foundation and the Nevada Arts Council provided funds for the residencies and this book; we are indebted to their generous support. Finally, a very special thanks goes to Jan Johnson for her ongoing commitment to the artists, their residencies, and publication of their work. Her energy and enthusiasm made this program a success.

Steven High, Director/CEO, Nevada Museum of Art

" *It was a privilege to give voice to some whose lives took me from the dailiness of routine to the irrefutable fact of their existence, which in some cases was no longer than that day.*"

—Shaun T. Griffin

WINTER IN PEDIATRICS
FIRST PLANTING

Poems by Shaun T. Griffin

SEPTEMBER 25, 2001

"I began the residency with trepidation: what will I do, how will I find a way into the pulse of the hospital? How will I transcribe the perfect declension of healing and pain? I did not know but began without answers. Like all who call this country home, I am reeling from the utter chaos of New York and Washington. My life is small. In some undefined way, this experience gives definition to more than darkness, for which I am grateful."

HOSPITAL JOURNAL

Drove down in rain clouds
to a clean, scrubbed earth,
sage almost worth smelling.
Inside the hospital, my tour
of memory, places not yet sutured:
pediatrics, oncology, intensive care—
weighted names that recall
the lens of human frailty.

Downstairs, the voices of children
drench the halls. I am grateful for
their screams, pure pleasure
a fortnight after horror
took us to seed. What voice
have we but the prodding child
to tempt the day from bed?

Upstairs, a father falls from his wrath.
His son waits in recovery,
mother flusters the couch with tears.

How do they hold what they loved?
I announce to no one, as if to skip
from the flag-laden halls, our fear.

OCTOBER 2, 2001

"Leaving the hospital, I drove toward Reno holding sunflowers for friends. At Mill and Wells, I swerved to the curb: a young man on his skateboard hit by a car, shaking uncontrollably in the street, the red pool below him. How could I have spent the morning in trauma and not seen such pain? I knew he would be lying in ICU when I returned, hoping, praying for a way out. The face I saw was our unfinished human face—the one we are learning to touch but still shy from. I hoped he would speak to me on my next visit. I hoped he would be alive."

IT WAS NOT BLAME

Of all the voices wishing flight
from their beds, the smallest dreams
at my side, head hutched in their flying hands,
the volley of sweet nameless faces
who push her back to this world
to crest the day without a tear,
that which slips from her eye,
child of the unfinished marriage.

It was not blame
who steered her young life over
the precipice, how we try
in grief's aftermath
to navigate the shallows of her life,
the rudderless work of mother,
slow, dreamless step-taking
to the other side
of autumn's waiting hand.

3

OCTOBER 9, 2001

"For almost forty-five minutes I sat bungling my Spanish with a mother and father who were praying their young daughter return to any life she had known. Dumbly, I sat shaving the silence. He asked how much my poem would cost, the one I would write for them. I laughed the dubious laugh of the poet undressed and insisted, 'Nothing, nothing. The hospital is paying for this.' Those words almost finished, he asked for help with his work card, his ticket to America."

"Again, paradox reared its head as I left the hospital—in the parrot store of all places. My son had run out of food for his cockatiel, and I stopped to buy a bag of seed. People were holding their parrots, petting them, loving them. Minutes before, I watched infants in the arms of volunteer caregivers, women who were doing the sainted work of bringing children into the world. I could not reconcile the distance from hospital to parrot shop. I had the limbs of premature infants in my arms."

MOSQUITOES

They squeak and squirt and squiggle
in my arms. Mosquitoes, they refuse
to go away. They link the room
with the suck and burp of bottles,
infants who writhe on the feather

that brought them to intensive care.
They swim in the palms of nurses
to slake the thirst of days under glass.
The names on the headboards
collect the first spots of milk.

For the whole of their short lives,
the words are gone, the vowels
slip to oxygen, the violet storm
of memory almost disguised
for the hours of lying alone.

OCTOBER 16, 2001

(En route to JFK)—"At our staff retreat yesterday, I sat beneath the aspens on Mount Rose, the leaves spilling like confetti. I thought of the young lives that would be touched by them, if only they could leave the hospital."

THE YELLOW LEAFLETS

Yesterday I sat in the yellow rain
of leaflets, the aspens shorn
by autumn's early wind.
But for the New York journey
to wish a poet well, I am

captive to the chocolate thieves
in intensive care, the hail of accents
from the registry nurses, the pediatric
scales tipped with ounces, and the
morning nod from Susan at the kiosk.

Tomorrow they will float from
my few weeks in a gown,
and I will have nothing
but leaves to remind in their absence,
the earthen lanterns spilling to ground.

Already I have become the arborist,
alone beneath his tree.

OCTOBER 23, 2001

"Yesterday I rode the elevator to the ground with a man who had just lost his daughter to an overdose. I had no words for the tears under his baseball cap. In the nursing station, a young mother, also a RN, upon learning of the father's loss, asked no one, 'Why do I do this job?' Later, I brought a Spanish newspaper to a mother trying to love her daughter back from the edge. I wanted to find some means of equaling the distance between us. Their voices trailed to the poem I tried to write in the autumn sun, tried but could not."

CHILD OF NO MOTHER

In the halls of the hospital
voices tremble—
the preemie
with the floating heart,
the boy whose body limped away,
the teen with a last prescription,
peeled to the ark of nothing.

Across town, an Irish peace activist
sings in juvenile hall
to fish the desire for guns
from their hands.

What would he sing to her,
she who fell
from the medicine cabinet?
Who missed her echo
across the wire?

In the elevator,
her father weeps
a prayer in our steel room
for the natural elevation
of the daughter who could not run.

OCTOBER 30, 2001

"I am slowly learning the alphabet of the hospital, putting sound to illness, story to passbook. I sat with a mother whose son was breathing from a life-saving machine. Across the hall, a homeless family hoped their young child would return with them. To where, I thought? Not the street, not the street. On this nearly last day of October, rain came once again to cleanse, to slip us all to shore."

THE TOIL OF CLOUDS

She lifts him to breathe
from the tube of clean air.
His eyes follow like pale blue stars,
fingers curled to the one
who resurrects feeling. On the window
the crayon telegraphs from school:

How are you?
We miss you in math, Come back soon.

She has waited with him for seven days.
It will be seven more before the rumor
of germ-work slithers from lungs.

A sixth week of dry autumn wind flinched to rain.
Today, he breathes from the toil of clouds.

NOVEMBER 6, 2001

"After finally feeling some comfort in pediatrics, I spent the afternoon with two remarkable seniors—in their homes, not in the wings of patient care. One of them was Nevada's first female pharmacist, the other a gardener unlike any I had met. Tomatoes, apples, squash, and seed pods were strewn throughout the yard. He left more vegetables on the ground than I have grown in my life. This from a man who could almost see."

ODE TO THE TILLER

Hale under the brim of his hat,
he yanked the feeling out of his good hand
but the Briggs and Stratton
wouldn't sputter the garden of uprooted vines.
He hooked his neck down-cylinder
like it was a cure
to rattle the piston with ether
and shook the four-cycle to the ground.

He knew tomorrow would bring blades
in the manure and wobbly roots
winding the earth, no vegetables for winter
but those few in the shed,
the butternut and over-large tomatoes,
so flush he thought them cheeks
to signal his neighbors
at close of harvest.

NOVEMBER 20, 2001

"Spent the morning in ICU with a wonderful caregiver. She made even the smallest act seem profound: speaking, breathing, swallowing. When she gave a man speech through a device the size of a quarter, she said, 'This is the most rewarding part of my job,' having learned through years of practice to comfort his family when all they wanted to do was cry."

ROOMS

I

What room do you come from,
child of the broken lung?

And you, hockey player
whispered open by a stroke?

The family gathered bedside,
the chorus singing father's name.

II

Husband of sixty years,
he lay in this place not two months ago.
He gestures under fluorescent light:
hematoma, pacemaker. She believes
him, but they are not words.

They idle the chords of the long married.
He intimates a kiss, a squeezed hand.
She rehearses the word for love.
It is the first word she will speak,
his name on her tongue since the 40s.

She regards the loss of time
to ordinary events as bead work,
like breathing or waiting for the weight
of blankets. This, behind the draped
outline of a man with her ring.

NOVEMBER 27, 2001

"Briefly followed the speech therapist on her rounds, found some 'old friends,' patients I met only last week, and one who miraculously could now speak. He would have the grace notes of parallel thinking and speech for the remainder of his days. He would not be sentenced to silence in middle age. Although I was merely a fragment in his hospitaled life, he found joy in our simple, simultaneous awareness of this fact, and he waved his good hand at my face, as if to say thanks. Returning to pediatrics, I kissed a good-bye to a young boy who would live in his house for the first time in his brief four months."

IN THE TENT OF MIRACLES

I have no words for your heart
already halved at four months.
You live in the tent of miracles,
sent from a family of teachers
and engineers who labor in fields
of fast food. Your eyes swim
between mother and uncle who waded
through two hospitals in two states
to waste the worry of dying.
Tú eres su milagro,

but you must know that—smallest of six
whose hands have yet to touch
the frost out the window,
the birch leaves cartwheeling to ground,
like you, Nestor, to wake
in a room of natural light and sound.
You are almost old enough to love
the hands that hold your breadth:
her hands, she of the old soil, she
who daily folds your heart in her arms.

DECEMBER 4, 2001

"I watched a stroke patient take his first steps today, just weeks after a clot shut him down. Nothing short of grace in his eyes. I keep hoping to see his wife. She must be so happy. They have no insurance. He is a futures trader. He goes to rehab in the next couple of days. I will visit him on my way down the hill. I will say small things. I will listen for his words to come back of their own volition."

OF FREEDOM'S GAIT

He signals to her for water and pain—
his athlete's heart threshes in failed flesh.
The questions swim to the surface:
Will he walk? How will I tell him?

There is no answer, but his
right leg lifts to her command,
and arm steadied to brace, then knee,
hip, the slow chemistry of steps
logged again for the first time,

motion unspent in surgery's attic.
His voice almost announces the slap
of feet to floor, and she who knows
the pivotal language of bones
tells him, *Great job, you did great,*

hands and feet reunited for the uneasy
tumble to floor, dizzy now
she lays him to pillows with the hint
of one good day on the court.

DECEMBER 11, 2001

"It has been three months since I woke to planes flying into buildings. All words stopped. Today, I am halfway through the residency. Soon I will visit my friend to see him take more steps. I did follow-up with the speech therapist today. We visited a former ICU patient. Above his bed, there were pictures of him fishing. He asked if I would write about him. I nodded and wished the poem could send him back to the Sea of Cortez."

IN THE ABSENCE OF WATER

Fisherman, your hand shook
like you were reeling tuna,
but it was not tuna, only fingers pushed
to yours under the tremor of blankets.
You almost asked, *Where do you fish?*
the first quiver of sound from a throat
closed to the memory of albacore and dorado,
and we climbed from the bilge of the boat:
water came quick to soothe.

Stay off the booze, you said, as if to forecast
the white fog of hospital linens where you
navigate old arms through saline
waters bulbing from skin, the pulse
not registering, and you left to the stern
of your metal ship, the freckles of family
anguished over the glass, a last fin
sprung from the rod, the echo of gills
and scales and salt from your lungs.

DECEMBER 18, 2001

"I have finally come to the hospital long enough to find friends, and friends of those taken early by grief's talons. I am grateful to know them. Even over this holiday I remember their struggle to do the ordinary and find myself not the poet, but the one without words. Each day they shape who I am, these people stopped by something other than old age. They remind me to kiss the light out my window."

DRIVING TO THE FOREST AFTER WORK

Before you were cut from the day,
you drove to the forest

ready to run—and running—
however still in the morphine night,

cross the cotton dressing,
disguise the erratic stitches

as if they were stars,
inch closer to family

gathered this Christmas
near the purple rings that rise

up your leg to a loft of pillows,
for what relief might come.

"It was my first day back at the hospital in three weeks. Nestor, the infant boy whose heart was damaged at birth, came back. Although I hoped never to see him on this floor again, I was relieved that he was not seriously hurting. His oxygen was low, but he was feisty. I sat with him for a long time, saying those foolish monosyllables, as if one or two of them found their way to his ears."

MONOSYLLABLES

Nestor, your hands
flood the crib
with movement.
Like your heart once halved,
you distract them
from the fallen
hemoglobin.

Your mother climbs
the icefall of months
with a cloth partition
between the space
of two beds,
as if it held
a day without nurses:

a day before
the red bulb
dimmed the center
of this room
and she forgot
the callus
of your imperfection.

JANUARY 15, 2002

"I sat with Nestor for about an hour today, listening to his breath rise and fall, the monitor beeping in the nursing station. Later I went to visit my friend in rehab. He's doing much better, although he and his wife face massive bills and uncertainty. Decisions about where and how he will live after this place bear down on them. I will tell my son he is drinking fluids without the powder to help him swallow. I will tell him he will go home soon. In pediatric rounds, they shared the story of the boy who woke from an overdose on the football field. How many boys—myself included—have wanted the strength to stay alive?"

WITHOUT ADOLESCENCE

Your parents, the ones who want
to ask how you drank cheap rum
on the football field

in the hope of waking
without adolescence—
they were ordinary, your parents.

They held nothing in the green fields
of chalk lines. They wanted something
other than glass to tarnish the night.

They wanted the flesh of one boy
before the swimming began,
before the angel of recovery

limped into the room and blew
you back to the question
they could not ask.

JANUARY 22, 2002

"I was in ICU and began talking to one of the nurses. She told me about this young man who had taken a bad slide down the mountain. His friends tried to find help, but they were out of bounds and lost. All of them, cold and whispering to loved ones…if I come back. I wanted to meet him, but he was heavily sedated to keep him out of pain. At least he will walk away from the hospital. I imagine he will cherish all of his days."

THE BREATH BEFORE QUIET

Snowboarder, you thought the moon
a white landscape to crest,
the tree-shadows, small men
who walked to the forest edge.
Your name is an old friend to cold,
where the lost pray the ridge top
will slide to the canyon mouth.
All thin fiberglass points you down

the cornice, shoots you over stone
to the final breath before quiet.
Your neck is collared to stitch
circumstance to feeling.
In the land of no snow, your hands
hold the mask of sensation.
Before dawn, they will point
to the forest beyond your room.

JANUARY 25, 2002

"I spent Friday talking with a wonderful young person who is waiting for a heart. How she finds the courage to live with such uncertainty, I do not know. I could not stop thinking about her. Sunday morning, when there was peace in the house, I sat by the fire in sunlight and wrote about her, and still, I could not define her existence: she lives as birds live—never far from that which sustains."

THE HEART DONOR

I

You whisper into the forest of small hearts,
the marriage of finite halves in your chest.
You wait for a call that will save—
the flight to surgeon who will seam skin
with the organ of another. The odds of undoing
are precise: for you to live, one must die
on a fingerprint, the muscle jigsaw to lungs.

You are a woman at the breast of another,
her face a diary of unfinished labor.
A collage of names awaits her—mother, worker,
woman who speaks with her unborn children—
the chemistry of waiting for the unknown,
as yet unloved, but she will wake you,
kiss the brow of your lithe frame
and answer with her life. She will rest one from two,
close your hands as you start to thank her
and follow to old age.

II

She who receives will not know how it came.
She will not know what car you were driving,
what word you spoke before breath entered for the last time.
She will name you mother and you will unfold in her
the wisdom of your half-life, the quizzical turntable
that found you donor, lifted from lungs that she might
always breathe your first word in thanks. There will be no silence
to commemorate the algorithm of pulse to pain.
She will fold a letter and wish it to arrive at your door,
but you will not be there. You will answer with your life—
and she become what each could not,
the metronome of two hearts undone.

17

JANUARY 29, 2002

"Pediatric rounds were tough today—I couldn't take much more sadness. An eight-year-old asthmatic was care-flighted to ICU in full arrest. They say he will be brain dead. His father gave him CPR for fifteen minutes before the ambulance arrived. Another infant has cardiomyopathy—he will need a heart soon. And a young foreign exchange student, raped in a small town. The staff was overwhelmed with sadness. They manage so much that is untenable. I needed to come outside to the warmth of a winter day."

THE UNWANTED COWBOY

It is the anniversary of Ghandi's death,
the sky has shorn all color but blue and
white stars below the halo of daybreak.

At the hospital, she perforates the weight
of him in her arms, the immigrant student
he stripped to no woman. She marks this day

with Ghandi's sadness, the taste
of flesh bent to dust in the new world.
I gather wood and think of her scaled to ribs—

what must she confide to the desert?
Her mouth is a moon for the loss of words,
hunched over the rim of the eastern sky.

FEBRUARY 12, 2002

"Work kept me from the hospital. Has it ever been any other way for artists? I could not answer but remembered my friends in peeds, that half-name to which I ascribe the daily saving of small lives. All through the day, the tiny telegraphs from patients and staff, hear me that I am, their faces a collage of recovery and silence. Again, I kiss the angel that made this journey possible."

THIS IS A CHILD

One day after I flew to a school
for children without houses,
there was no solace
in pediatrics
where the rumor
of small lives persists.
What do they revive
for the regimen of daily revival—
these cradle marks
the slight body
forfeits for the tail
of oxygen
from a machine?
Like those without
the whim of shelter,
this is a child,
a mouth suckled
on the full breast of dissent
in a colony of new faces
five floors above the earth.

FEBRUARY 19, 2002

"I held Nestor's hand for thirty minutes yesterday. I don't know if he will make it. His face is swollen, and he looks like he is slipping from this life. His parents are tired and losing their resilience. My friend who had the stroke did a TV spot with the doctor who saved him to promote the doctor's inter-arterial procedure. Medicine, I did not know its name."

THE DOO-WOP COKE BOTTLE QUARTET

Veteran, you fly solo in the turbulence
of another war—but this wound
is not the gift of an enemy.
There are five pale stars moaning
the streets of cheap, colorless wine
that stings the voice you doo-wopped
from Coke bottles with friends,
your thin frames balanced on the curb.

A breathing tube gurgles the room,
and she takes your pulse, not knowing
what wound to redress. She is
all you have—caretaker, nurse,
whose single affirmation
requires nothing of your silence.
In a volley of streetlight, you wake
the worry of bottles, and she remains.

FEBRUARY 26, 2002

"I drove to the school where Nestor's mother works to talk with her, see how she is doing. Ironically, it is the same school where I had worked as a poet, so there were many friends, even a former student who is now a counselor. His mother was grateful to have some other person in this long ordeal, some other voice to reconstruct the sorrow. At breakfast, her husband said they have opened his entire body, what more can be done to save him? I could only hold her on the playground."

WATCH HIM DISAPPEAR

Nestor, each day you disappear
into the folds of medicine,
your throat tubed to oxygen,
the lemon liquid taped to your chest.
I touch your fingers and your eyes
perk open. You have found new stories
to believe in. Some wishes
you spell with your small hands.

Outside, a dove calls to no one from the spruce.
I think of the monitors that engineer
your hours clipped to bedside,
how you blur the air of intimacy
to feel mother's love. She is not
in the room, but hears you always.
The blue scripture of veins pinch her chest,
the imperfect blossom of your heart.

She empties her purse to call someone,
anyone, to the only moment—*now,*
the calendar of imperfect things.

MARCH 5, 2002

"I left the hospital to see my friend who is recovering from a stroke (both spouses are recovering—he from a stroke, and she from the loss of so many things). Finances are killing them. I wanted to do something to pry them out of their isolation. It was the end of a day when many I had grown close to had only failure to console them."

AFTERMATH

You live with the uncertainty of checkbooks.
Your wife peels from the ledger of zeroes.
This because a barbaric clot
closed the flow of oxygen for a millisecond.
The doctors reassure, function will return.
But you are not so sure, exiled to the jobless
routine of family who wait
for one star to sneak from the clouds.
Her hands nearly pull with promise, this woman

you married a half-life ago, and now the reeds
of failure sprout from the desk—before creditors
and God, you ask forgiveness for the caprice
of your fallen limbs. There is no
place for the gathering of body-wishes
in this house where you scale flesh
for signs of new life and light candles
to signify the points of stars that illumine
what they, without clots, cannot see.

MARCH 12, 2002

"It has been almost six months since I started the residency. It is coming to an end. I can't imagine these days without this experience. One of the respiratory therapists took me to ICU this morning where we met a young man with muscular dystrophy. His mother, bedside, seemed as if she had been through every illness with him."

"There was a rough-skinned hawk circling outside the window during pediatric rounds. Rounds were almost fun today, we were in the peeds ICU waiting room—warm and light. Soon I will go to my friend who had the stroke and hope his life is not too stressed."

THE IRIS BALLET

The light over Mount Rose combs the irises
on the sill. Your mother grows twelve
varieties of the violet rainbow.
She has given twenty-two years
to unwind your body. Under the blankets,
your feet twist to cloth,
braid the tubes of aquarium sounds.

There are four hands to clear your airway
of the words *I can't breathe,* your face
a pillow for lying under silence.
You draw stories with their hands,
and she holds your legs, says *don't worry*
as the pulse races, says *your friend
will come soon* to trick clocks into believing

tomorrow, says your MD is genetic,
passed *from me,* as if she could take
the consonants from your lungs.

MARCH 19, 2002

"Spent the morning talking with a wonderful gardener. He had more soil secrets than I had poems. Upstairs, in peeds ICU, lies a young snowboarder who hit his head when he jumped too far. He may not make it. Fourteen years old. Last year his mother died. I smiled at the father—it was all I could do."

A SEASON NOT YET SOWN

Mourning doves coo from the spruce.
Upstairs he lies in the tent of angels.
There is no way down, the long journey
to earth. I could only console—
the living have their job.

Tomorrow is the first day of spring.
A gardener tells of his tomato exploits—
he is nearly free in the soil.
The father upstairs would spade cement
for one good year with his son.

Soon the gardener will plant the first crops—
Spanish peanuts, strawberries, and collard greens.
If there is no kill-frost, no caprice
to lance the roots from darkness,
they will bear in one hundred twenty days.

A season not yet sown for fathers and boys.

He invites me to his garden. I may go
to his field of unfinished greens.

MARCH 26, 2002

"I don't want this experience to end. I'll try to find a way to continue. I was in peeds with Nestor for 20 minutes and then introduced myself to the father of the young snowboarder. He holds his son's leg softly. I think I would be doing the same—wishing for a miracle. I can't imagine his anguish, and I hope when I return in two weeks that he has better news. Their neurologist is up against a wall—the choices are not easy. Either way is danger. I called my friends (the stroke patient and his wife). They're very sick, so I could not visit them. This is my last 'official' day. I will write in the sun."

AT WINTER'S END

I have come to winter's end,
have brushed the lives of patients
throughout this subterranean globe,
been witness to that which endures—
the holy freedom of human life—
and that which destroys—
the makeshift angel of death.

We have no reason to chart death's course,
and so choose the infant's pale arms,
the elder's docile arms, but choose,
nonetheless, to stay alive.

I have watched healing under
a microscope and found no cell
but the human, have pushed blood
from its face and still blood returned.
All this we do that one may live,
and I am the storyteller—
they bring hands to this work.

"I've approached my paintings with this intent: to convey that fragile moment when time suspends itself; one blink of the eye implanting a scene permanently on the consciousness before time once again resumes its perpetual task. In some pieces a person's presence still lingers briefly on the air, as though the soul left a whisper of an impression on the moment."
—Sharon Maczko

SHARON MACZKO

Paintings from the Washoe Medical Series

STEPS TOWARD RECOVERY

On my second day at Washoe Medical Center, I spoke at length with the fiancé of a woman who had sustained injuries to her neck, pelvis, and head in a car accident, and was still receiving treatment in ICU after ten days. I was so taken with the love and adoration her fiancé's words and actions expressed for her, but it was when he explained to me that he had learned that there were many "steps" she would have to undertake toward her recovery that a mental image formed in my mind of a stairway—stair steps that would serve as a metaphor for the steps to recovery.

After more consideration, I decided to use a ladder instead of a stairway (an apple-picking ladder, incidentally, which I thought possessed more character than a regular ladder.) The two lowest rungs are broken, so theoretically it would take strength and willpower to begin climbing the ladder by stretching to the third rung; this symbolizes the strength and willpower necessary for a patient to overcome those first few crucial hours or days following serious injury.

The ladder sits on a dirt road, and in the vista, beyond the sagebrush, rises a huge thunderhead cloud. This aspect of the painting came to me when the gentleman spoke of his fiancé as possessing incredible physical strength, which she would most certainly have to rely upon in her steps to recovery. A thunderhead cloud has always appeared to me as an immensely powerful object, constantly building upon its own strength and growing in intensity healthier, and more capable, so I felt it was the perfect symbol of her strength.

This painting stands as a tribute to the hope and perseverance of anyone in the act of recovery.

Sharon Maczko, *Steps Toward Recovery*, 1999, transparent watercolor, 36" x 25.75", from the *Washoe Medical Series*.

AN AFTERNOON IN NEUROLOGY

The Neurology Unit is an area of the hospital that could be described as experiencing both tragedies and miracles on an almost daily basis. It is an understatement to say that some patients and their family and friends will spend an emotionally difficult time here. Confused patients are trying to recover and rehabilitate while their family members are trying to adjust to the temporary (or sometimes permanent) changes in their loved ones. During the steps to recovery, patient's can be either violent or performing embarrassing or humiliating acts upon themselves. When heart-rending drama is at its peak, by what measure are we to attempt to cope? Contemplate that and consider confronting these tumultuous extremes on a daily basis, year after year, and you may comprehend what it must be like to be a nurse working in Neurology. The staff informed me that by making a conscious effort to let the miracles outweigh and lessen the effects of the tragedies, they are able to approach their job with gratification and enjoyment.

This painting is a conglomeration of events, described to me by the nurses, that took place at varying times in the Neurology Unit. Each doll conveys a story and represents the patients who, to my perception, are for the time being "changed" people; play-acting their lives in an inconceivable drama. This painting is not meant to make fun of the patients, but rather to illustrate circumstances that the nurses contend with.

The staff and nurses endure much while working on this floor, from angry, frustrated family members to dangerous situations. They should be saluted for their tenacity, perseverance, and their positive outlook.

Sharon Maczko, *An Afternoon in Neurology*, 1999, transparent watercolor, 11" x 30", from the *Washoe Medical Series*.

PAWNS

Many apprehensions had manifested in my thoughts as I undertook the Artist In Residence program at Washoe Med; some were silly, others stood ground. One concern was how would I react and how competently would I be able to cope were I to witness some terrible human tragedy, which I was sure I would face on a daily basis. Of course, that perception was extreme but I did, nevertheless, find myself in a situation that left a dramatic impression on me.

I had chosen one day to visit the Pediatrics Unit, and eventually wandered into Pediatric Intensive Care. I became drawn into a family crisis where a young child had been injured, not only because I was literally trapped in a corner of the ICU and unable to exit when emotions came to a staggering peak but because I felt their passion so heavy in the air. As I stood there trying in vain to choke back tears, I found myself in that situation I had so dreaded: witnessing a very real human tragedy endured by a family of people who were complete strangers to me. On reflection I realized that what struck me profoundly was not the sadness or regrets of these people, but the fact that my presence there had completely pulled me into their situation, and I felt as strongly as they of our impotence in our ability to change life's circumstances.

I longed to reach out and hug them, to try and calm and soothe them, but I felt the invisible barrier of some existing moral standard that said I could not enter any further into this family's private troubles. In the painting, a window is used to illustrate this point—transparent enough to see a clear picture of the drama, but an impediment in affording me access to reach out to them.

The next day the child's mother related to me that she felt she was not fulfilling her role as his mother because she had to leave him to the care of the nurses; she didn't feel in control anymore. I illustrated this point by portraying the parents as puppets, as though some unseen entity was pulling the strings and in control of the situation. They play a game of chess, because sometimes it appears as though life is a game of pure chance, with all the risks and strategies inherent in the journey of our existence. And what does the future hold for this family; do they choose from what's behind door number 1, 2, or 3? Each day is a gamble; you hope fervently that you've made the right decisions.

Sharon Maczko, *Pawns*, 1999, transparent watercolor, 17" x 22", from the *Washoe Medical Series*.

"What startled me most was that art could come from the wellspring of birth and death and life-saving experience that I was exposed to in the residency. A fellow poet ascribed this to the drama of the hospital. I doubted his explanation then and do so now. This was an art of weekly discovery; I never knew what would happen when I arrived. I was grateful for the chance to disappear, to become some other person in that place of healing."
—Shaun T. Griffin

SECOND HARVEST

Poems by Shaun T. Griffin

FEBRUARY 18, 2003

"My first day back at the hospital—nine months after leaving. The peed's staff welcomed me warmly. It was good to see all of them again. They're still as dedicated, still as caring. I tried to find my friend, the stroke victim's wife who now works at the hospital, but she didn't answer her pager. Later when I was visiting a friend's father in ICU, she found me and shared the unbelievable news: after all the two of them had been through, her husband had gone off the deep end. She was devastated, and I could not respond—incredulous in the middle of ICU. It would be the second such conversation I would have—Nestor, the baby with whom I sat with in pediatric ICU—left this world in August. I almost believe it was a good thing to be saved from the misery of a life entwined in tubes. So the reckoning begins—we come to life as sacred and let it go as no less sacred."

THE RECORD OF HANDS

In nine months I have not touched
these hands; they are worry stones:

my neighbor drove forty miles to fetch
a Valentine flower and rolled his truck;

a co-worker's husband waived off
rehab in a downtown motel.

They mimic the inchoate stares of lying
without love. The reasons do not lie down.

My neighbor pulls oxygen to his mouth,
my co-worker shelters her daughter

from the blaze of neon in the sky. Friends,
they cannot answer the persistent absence

of who they are: hands closed to mine,
what the priest calls the stain of living.

Have they any other living? In the time
a child gestates, I have not held its shadow.

FEBRUARY 27, 2003

*"Returned to the hospital today feeling dark—like the clouds
overhead. It is Thursday, not my normal day. I came to sit
in on the cancer support group—an incredible room full of
survivors, teachers, and healers. Remarkable humanity.
Some who struggled to say 'I'm alive,' and some who could not
muster those words. Voices that were stronger than almost any
voice outside, for theirs was pushed to air by faith, a tremulous
desire to become witness to the questions."*

WITNESS TO QUESTIONS

She waits in a dressing gown—beyond
the odorless white of biopsy and diagnosis.
Her son wants to know if she will change,
asks if she will have "wooden boobs."

In the support group, they welcome the survivor's
laugh, measure the consequence of a day
without suffering. The witness to questions
comforts what medicine cannot.

She breathes a memory into the air:
"I am alone with two children—
after the hospital, I need the day to go on."

MARCH 3, 2003

*"Went to peed's rounds today. Slowly getting back into the swing
of things. Two new cases of meningitis—a word I thought gone to
history. Tried to find my neighbor's father, but they have moved
him off-site to a rehab facility. Ran into my other neighbor in the
morning. She seems well, if wondering what to do. I paged my
friend who works here, and she seemed happy but still filled with
anger at all that had transpired with her addled husband. How to
let a loved one go?"*

SISTER TO THE VINE

for Chelise

She is fallen from the vine of their lives,
mother and father who, but for the tubes
that spider her arms, name this day hers.
A near-woman now, she is the daughter
of many tissues, the girl who knots
flesh with her eyes—quivers what is
expected like sand after water.
She recreates herself with the halo

of a gesture, finds the circle of family
in the mountains beyond the room.
For the ones who listen, she has a voice:
it is the ephemeral touch of sound to skin,
her lightening sound that will not go away.
She murmurs the fits of staying, of lying
bedside for what she will become, sister
to the vine, so many lives has she led.

MARCH 11, 2003

"Spent the morning in the gym with one of the occupational therapists. She was working with a young boy who had been hit by a car. It was so painful to watch him try to move. He kept repeating the words 'ow-ee, ow-ee, mommy help, mommy help.' The therapist was a natural healer. I want to try and paint the boy sitting on the mattress in the gym. Maybe tonight. It was so hard for him to lift the rings to the cone (one of the exercises she had him doing). I thought of my own son, his age, and how each of us navigates the land of needles, some never knowing their final touch."

GORDON GLOWING ON THE SHEET

Her hands slide a boy not quite from the chair.
She teases the good arm to chin, closes
his knuckles to a traffic cone.

In the blue-mat rehab room, she stretches
the sound of *Mommy, ow-ee* with balloons
for his thirteenth birthday.

They celebrate the pendular rhythm of up
and down, squeeze the cone for safety
like the drawings of doctors.

Tomorrow he flies to the land of free movement,
Another hospital, she baritones,
and maybe snow like this—

signals his arm to the window, the slim
vane that points at wind and chance
to risk a day of touch.

MARCH 18, 2003

"Spent the morning with the rehab therapist. What a soothing healer. We tried to get a young motocross rider from his bed into the bathroom. His leg was so badly broken he could hardly move. But she is so good with people, she was able to maneuver him into the bathroom. I didn't think we'd get him there. He and I talked a lot—he's an artist. A resilient soul, despite extreme pain, he's still persisting. Then I went and saw a co-worker's daughter. It was a fine morning in peeds.

The hospital was actually a relief from the vagrant worry of work and the world. I was really disturbed last night by all that had been said about Iraq. This morning, coming down, I saw a mountain bluebird, a sign of hope against the sky. Like the coyote and the peregrine over the weekend, the wild persists."

LAST NIGHT WE WERE TOLD WAR IS IMMINENT

Sleepless, I left for the hospital—
the desert of others awakened to dust.
I could not repair to the dreamless and
saw a mountain bluebird: our bird of paradise.
We live where wind eats bristlecone stumps,
where no water sprouts from stone,
where snowflakes in the March night
come as memory of a time before this.

In an eastern room I sat with him—
his bike tipped to dust in the Lovelock desert.
In weeks the swelling will go down,
skin grafts appease the darkness of his leg.
By the time he returns to ride, the bluebird
will have flown its sage perch, the desert of others
scrubbed silent. How like a bluebird
is the patina of skin without shrapnel.

MARCH 25, 2003

*"Spent the morning with the young rider who broke his leg racing. Really
enjoy talking to him—he's a great kid. So much of myself in him. He had
skin-graft surgery earlier in the week—hope it takes. He'll find out in a
couple of days. I'll try to stop by tomorrow or Thursday to see how he's
doing. The young rider wanted the poem I wrote last week, my notes were
still on top of it. I hope it doesn't ruffle feathers. It's funny, I would never
have dreamt the small tug of words would perk up a feisty adolescent.
Saw the recovering cancer patient too—playing Nintendo with the kids
in peeds. He was so much like the young boy he was playing with—you'd
hardly know he was recovering from cancer."*

LETTER TO JR

Today his wing is splinted with new skin.
He moves from chair to bed with the ease
of one who has straddled two wheels.
The room swims with diversions and
books mother brought from school.
We trade hoots about Steinbeck—
what the dust gave the Joads,

the first draft his last.
I am uneasy reading a poem,
apologize for its nearness to war, not him.
He smiles, tells me of the watercolor
in the studio of flowers and loved ones.
If the skin takes, I will hear him
in the pines, heavy on the throttle home.

APRIL 1, 2003

*"Spent the morning with my young motorcycle
friend. Read him the poem I wrote last week.
It's still in draft form, but it seemed to cheer
him up. We went to the stairs to try and
walk. It's so difficult for him. Afterward, his
leg throbbed—he was in real pain. I showed
him a few of the watercolors from our journey.
The occupational therapist was great with
him. I think she could work in the snow
and still exude warmth that only patients
understand. I saw my friend at lunch, and it's
still pretty rough trying to find the balance on
her own.*

*The next day I returned to the hospital, and
the young rider had just been told he needed
more surgery. He and his mother were
devastated. I tried to say something but could
not. I was useless. When I left, he asked me
to leave the poem for his mother. In all his
pain, it was the last thing I expected."*

WORDS FOR THE MAN I KNEW

It is the morning of his return.
My son shakes when he sees him,
my daughter leans into the house of doubt.
In the middle of that house I lay down,
adrift in the mouth that betrayed this first April day.

My home is an empty room. I live where
the day is ordered by the absence of his hands.
The children and I eddy at the turntable of regret—
it is not enough to wish him his weekly motel room.

We visit the memory of him, of us before the echo
of our life together sputtered to its silent end.
Now the partial family is ours. We ring the table
with place mats—one for each, sturdy in our chairs.

We remember grief's wineglass and set a serving
to scotch the ill wind in this house. When
there is a knock, we turn the blinds to fend
this first day of April that once was ours.

APRIL 8, 2003

"Went to rounds this morning, then left for a fund-raising event at an exclusive resort. So much opulence filled with impatient people. One of the homeowners said to a contractor, 'I have to be here six weeks of the year. I want everything perfect.' Dropped off a proposal, then came back to visit the young rider. He's not doing very well. He hasn't recovered from the surgery. Drowsy, nauseated, in pain. I'm worried about him. They were talking about the possibility of him losing his leg this morning. I had hoped to read him Grapes of Wrath, *but he's too out of it. Then a volunteer walked in, and a friend I hadn't seen in at least a year. I really like all the crew in here—incredible people."*

READING STEINBECK TO JR

It's a book of dust dug in the floorboards,
a last green sprig before the Rockies,
what never got said on the Divide—

We failed them dumb farmers.
He asks if I understand the prologue,
long enough already, and no drama to relay.

I understand the helicopter morning
he found the sage empty of daylight.
His face is pale, the lips have not spoken

freely in days. He lifts the fever-whisper
of post-operative waking: *But they wanted
to come west, didn't they?* I don't answer—

the small hand survives migration
and the burden of a story not yet finished.

APRIL 29, 2003

"Rounds were short today. There must not be many patients. The boy we played with last week went home yesterday. I brought my paints to share—I'll try to paint his face today. I feel rested from my trip back east, not anxious to speed back up. The transition from poet to my 'other life' is a shock—I'm not a fancy writer here. I'm very much in the thick of things that are not always easy. But I would tire of the former and need the balance, the multiple lives we lead.

The head nurse said I can bring a poem to the nurses' station, so I'll try to do that each week. In conversation, I learned that a friend who works in the hospital had horrendous surgery. I don't know what her life will be like after this."

AFTER SURGERY

for S.

Today, a young man asked for food
at the hospital. I was without money,
having just learned of your surgery:
from you, they took the taste of food.

This, to stay alive in the bare wire
of living beyond cancer. There are
no rules in this moment without choice.
You raise a lung to receive loved ones,

and the sour breath endures the flight
from testimony to patience—
you have come to the arbor's edge
and here must tend a new field.

The daffodils will persist, the daylight
enfold what has become woman. I think
of the hundred fields tended by women
who turn the subtle over and over in their palms

to remake the morning for each other, for
the long white indifference at the door.

MAY 6, 2003

"Slept deeply and came down to rounds. Feeling like a part of the team in peeds. I still don't know enough medical terminology to understand everything, but I understand the complexity of caring for critically ill kids. Each staff member plays an integral role. This morning, I went with two physical therapists to peeds ICU to work with a young boy. He could hardly stand, there were so many tubes hanging from his neck and body. But still, he was calm, peaceful as they worked with him."

IN THE ROOM OF FIRST LIVING, FIRST DYING

I

The tubes swarm from your body—
these are your limbs below the bed.
You have lived long with them—
they are nearly natural: the suck of fluids
to voice the one constant sound: I am.

Today, you stood on legs in her arms,
the bright shoes not yet creased, until weary,
the halt of sound and your breath tapered.
You swung the hammer to xylophone
and drew a stick man before it disappeared.

She washed your face and combed the auburn hair,
whisked the signs for cookie, good job, and want.
Her hands were stenciled at your waist.
She laid you back to bed and folded
the argument of medicine at your side.

II

There were months in this room last year
with another who spoke through machines.
His life was not alone—he was loved
by each who came through this door.

I pinched his finger to know him,
to witness a child at play in the fields
of medicine. I have come to this room
as sanctuary, where each who lies here

is more than their one or two lives—
they are scores of palms against the glass
that separates sterile from ordinary.
And having seen the hands, I release them

to the house of children, where they may
burrow in the palms of first feeling.

45

MAY 13, 2003

"The physical therapist and I played with a toddler for a good part of the morning. Today he was sitting in his bedside car when we arrived—tubes and all! We hooked him up to a portable oxygen bottle and walked around the floor. When we got to the fish tank, a nurse looked through the other side: she looked like a giant green and yellow mermaid. The therapists are really easy to be with. My co-worker's daughter is back here again. The rhythms of existence at the hospital. Even in peeds ICU, there is laughter. There is playfulness and spontaneity. In a funny way, the young patients cheer their nurses up—when they gesture or smile or acknowledge their presence. How dependent we are on human affirmation. Leaving the hospital, I saw a friend who lost her husband to cancer—younger than I am. She seems all right. I don't know how."

PROGRAMMER

for Bill

Days ago, he flew the dirt in his Landcruiser,
wrote programs for the tunnel of ideas.
Into the house of living things, he wedged
a presence: she knew what this time meant.

When the first rain came, the dust bloomed
in a field of other tasks and the waiting began.
Once this day was over, the rain settled among
the small hands of their son. *My father*

may not make it—he needed no translation.
For the next many months, they waited
at the door of questions. The furious doctoring,
the full light of weather about to descend.

I have wished for reasons to explain the person
who sleeps at the edge of failed health. The swing
from here to hour's end lies under his tongue—
the life-word *I*, a wafer that disappears.

JUNE 10, 2003

"Returned from Alaska late Sunday night, then started a full two days to now: the Arts Council conference call at 9 Monday—which I completely forgot, followed by a long day of prep for the board meeting. Today I went to peeds—it was great to see everybody. They were friendly and jocular. One of the physical therapists wanted to see the photos and paintings from the Coastal Plain. At the end of rounds, I heard the news: my young motorcycle friend is back in the hospital and will have his leg amputated tomorrow. I spent the morning with him. The physical therapist who has spent so much time with him was moving his leg—the one that will be removed. I had no words except to tell him he had much to teach us. The two staff who dressed his wounds also came over. He was scared and teary. God, he's such a courageous kid."

THE WAITING DAY

I

After thirty-nine days in this healing place,
you return to a room on the west wall—
unannounced. Absent sun, you sleep
before waking to this once-fulsome limb,
close the shade to what lies in your path,
and let go of the clean white suffering
scraped from the tissue of resurrection.

II

For sixteen years you leaned on this knee,
and she has come to bend its stiff presence,
teach the leg to begin the warm confluence
of movement on stairwells and escalators. This
is the woman who diagrams the city of lost
nerves. For all your brief stay, she teases
them to health in the hallways of doctors and
nurses who coach the wound vac' through
one more night of miserable pulsing.

She dreams of the daily answer to your writhing,
the end to questions that break and break
at your bedside. She is the dissolution of fear
in the house of new limbs, the silence that lifts
you to reach for the earth of home.

JUNE 23, 2003

"Went to rounds yesterday and was deeply moved by their magnanimous concern for the well-being of those infinitely small lives in their care. Spent an hour with my motorcycle friend talking about how it would go when he returned home. Saw another old friend downstairs—she's much happier. I think she's put the sorrow of her loss behind her. Walking out of the hospital, I looked up to see a woman from the cancer support group. What she said was astonishing—just weeks prior, she did not know if she would live, and today she stood before me like a rose that blooms to announce, I am alive."

SURVIVOR

a found poem for S.

It's hard to get used to the idea

of not dying—

should I renew

this subscription,

plan for Christmas?

For six months,

the killing cloud rode my flesh

to a last, prescient lie:

I might live

to abide its sorrow.

Today, I am a woman restored—

if not to health,

to the idea of tomorrow

without death.

JUNE 24, 2003

"Had a full morning at the hospital—rounds were very good but hard. The pathos sometimes overwhelms. A young girl was hit by a car and had head injuries. Her father wanted coffee, but he had no money and the office machine was broken. The nurse felt bad for him and said in rounds, almost parenthetically, 'I'm not going to say anything. I've always been wrong in the past,' meaning, she would give no negative prognosis about the girl. What we learn by listening to the resilience of young lives cannot be recorded."

THE SENSE OF LIFE IN HER ARMS

for Kenna

She lies in the ruin of her small frame.
No one saw the car shoot the crosswalk.
The woman she may become peeks
from the transparent lace of trauma. Her father
struggles for coffee. In the lounge, a nurse
confides, *I cannot say a thing—children*

recover. Out of the hope she kindled
in nursing school comes the girl to ask:
will the apple fly to my unwashed hands,
to which she draws on the window, a smile.
Down the hall, two nurses curl the bed
and read to a boy who pronounces a wisp

of his name. There is no requirement
for this desire to start over, to restore
the soiled ground on which a child stands.
A nurse yields to the unspoken,
the tender of something unsaid,
the buoyancy of young hands.

JULY 8, 2003

"Went to rounds—heard the damndest stories, all the convoluted rhetoric of those who don't or can't care anymore. Thankfully, the staff has been through this a hundred times, and they roll with it, trying still to administer care. My little friend with the congenital disabilities went to another hospital, and my motorcycle friend finally went home. I miss him but know he is happiest in the pines and can now begin to live again."

PLAYGROUND

A tree of heaven hangs over the empty swing.
The courtyard walls are stacked with rooms
to the sun: summer is the steady whine
of cold air. A larger voice hales beyond
the hospital—the daily friction lost to the living.

Here, the order is recovery, no less a monastic
order than first script. This morning in rounds,
the best minds drawn to the flesh worried
the voice dry: *he will not wake, she was touched
inappropriately*, as if the resplendent

knowledge of trees stood the questions
to offer the morning under shade, and no one
heard their layered hands reach
the courtyard to answer the littlest in their care
who must never stop the breath begun.

JULY 15, 2003

"Came down to peeds—rounds were funny. I think the nurses had had it—seen and heard all the excuses. The mom who schedules the care conference four times, the grandmother who shows up to visiting drunk, on and on. Humor is what keeps them alive. Hung out with the physical therapists—one was working with an obese boy with a trach. Tough to watch, anticipate what to do. My other friend in physical therapy walked with an old man with many problems, mostly just trying to stand and breathe and communicate. I tried to imagine slipping into that land—the loss of recognition—and could not. Called my motorcycle friend yesterday—he came down for his wound change and sounded good."

FATHER TO AN IMAGINARY GRANDSON

With each swallow of orange juice
      you migrate from the easy chair.

The caregiver wanders eight feet
      for you, faint, dressed for the visit

with your child and her children.
      Your grandson kicks from the stroller—

he wants to ride your chair—
      his two years are extant.

What divinity regards such loss:
      you have no name for him—

he suspends the chart in the hall:
      today, there are no memories.

What the years engraved,
      don't matter, grandpa,

as if to say, you got me
      to pinch death's indifference.

LUNCH WITH THE TRABAJADORAS

"Later, I went outside and had lunch with the trabajadoras. They let me sit with them and before long we were talking in Spanish. Of all the people I have met here, it is they who know this place intimately, for they must Clorox its every inch."

Chica mala sends her friends the signal—
he speaks Spanish—*¿Te quieres un poco?*
No, no, se puedo—voy a mi casa.

In that moment, the hospital is varicose:
the floors and railings they sweep and dust
to keep the young and not so young

from dying. A family of five
share this table when the sun permits—
the rattle of Span-gles over dinero,

puro dinero. They eat the lunch hour
with incantations until
chica mala relents and lets me in,

as if I could choose to leave
the piecework of women in the brown
and white far north of Nevada.

JULY 22, 2003

"Rounds were quiet today—many people were gone. My physical therapist friends weren't working with the kids in pediatrics, so I followed one of them to her other patients. We held the arms of a middle-aged man who was learning to walk again. He was pleasant and without visitors. We returned to the room and another man, older, was talking to us as if we were family. Perhaps we were."

THE PATIENT

for P.

How is it you come to him—as one
fallen through grief's door, supine
from the months spent at the bed

of your spouse? Not long ago
you remembered the chosen
and were not among them. Today

you reach for the torso of his body,
the man in your care. There is no room
for the weight of death, of what remains

beyond the hospital. Your odyssey
led you to care for those like the man
you loved, and he awaits your palm:

the patient in the room of many leaves.
It is July outside, and summer may yet
arrive in this bouquet where he lives.

Without you, the room would flake
to dust, and there lie the two men
who stood recovery

and must recover still.
This is flesh starting over, the thread
of movement in watery limbs.

"Came to rounds exhausted—a full day of preparation for a class after two weeks of intensive writing. And here, that labor means nothing. I am here to listen, pay attention, reveal the vein of health and lost health, and turn back to my life when the day is over. But there is also stasis here, an expectation of healing, which is what sustains the thousand hands that touch the human back from the edge of lying down. I am grateful for the hours in this place, the fusing of light and dark."

WAKING IN THE HOSPITAL

I

Awake in too many places, I pushed
the tethers to their furthest ends:
to the roll call of telegrams in pediatrics,
which abruptly begins the waking—
the ritual of repair in a score of children.

A southern nurse and a new doctor converge
on the tendrils of chronic pain. We defer:
the reason for rounds is patience:
stop the splintered cells and
piece from the circadian, recovery.

I rule out the obvious with my smirk:
death is the doorman in movies.
The children have never met him.
They open books with rag dolls
and read as if we understood.

II

Lifted from her car by sons older than I,
by men stripped of reason for her care,
a mother presses the door. Her husband
watches, his white flesh tilts on the walker.

I remember the artist's chairs we oblige in time:
the stroller, the school desk, the cubicle,
and the laziest before this wheelchair she falls into—
evidence of a life born to more than chairs.

Soon other sons will lift flesh from the crib
of a car to climb the stairwells of healing,
and they may not find the precise
caliper to measure this pouring of a life

into the next-to-last chair that reclines
to the growth of lavender overhead.

AUGUST 12, 2003

"Spent the morning with my young friend with many congenital problems. Had a really good time with him—he's so loved in this place. Many of the nurses spent time with him. Soon I'll follow a chaplain around the hospital, like I'm part of the landscape here today. It's a good thing. This is the beginning of my last month here. The poem I posted today helped to close some wounds. I never dreamt a poem would perform a function beyond the natural relevance of art."

IN THE CHAPLAIN'S SHADOW

She's a frequent flyer—in and out
of the hospital, her dialysis a swim
to land with the ebb and flow of fluid.

This is my friend, she begins, *a poet—
I think of poets as prophets.* In the haze
of recovery, the woman stirs a hello

from her tongue. I join their hands
in prayer and do not understand
the weight upon either woman.

Seized by the order of the cross,
the chaplain is like belief—her cloth
confounds the heart without hope.

I remember the Greek Orthodox
symbol tiled at our feet in Naxos,
how it held the incantation

of belief to stone, wisdom which
becomes prayer to the patient. I watch
her hand in the palm of sorrow,

the flesh to whom she vows relief.
We are kin to loss, but we are not lost—
she confides and closes her visit.

THE SEASON OF BURNING

for D. and K.

"I should look up the roots of yesterday: it cannot possibly contain all that took place. I had a really good morning in rounds, then went to visit the firefighter who lost his spouse to a freak accident and severely injured his leg. My neighbor and his children were there, and many others. The fireman is still grieving—they had just married. I can't imagine what sorrow lies in wait for him. And still, he was worried about all those gathered to support him."

You are the first whisper of rejuvenation.
You emerge from heat like a bird from a flue,
even as the flame consumes, you move in the wind

to extinguish. Just yesterday, she walked to a store,
lost balance and the wind took her, took all you shared,
but lying in this hospital bed, you rise to cheer friends

who fight fire. You have never left the season of burning.
Your eyes pester the dark light. The flowers at your bedside
are tall trees, shelter from wind that blew her down. As they turn

from the confluence of hands that kill fire, others come to ring
the symbol of survival. Your life is edged with trauma and boredom—
between the two extremes is the watery light in your eyes,

the wonder beneath the heat that permits you to navigate a forest
of endless ash, a moment of breath-saving, the human wick
lit in disbelief. Your gift to them must finally allow for quiet—

what you intimate will not be spoken: the risk is the work, the wild
into which you freely step, imploring them to silence, those who wish
it could be otherwise, and still there is no silence: the fire remains.

AUGUST 27, 2003

"Woke early to see Mars this morning—the paper said the planet was in the southwest sky at dawn. It looked like a giant streetlight. Mars, the Roman god of war and agriculture. Before going to the hospital, I spoke on the public radio station about the residency. Some of my friends at the hospital listened, which was a good thing because the interview was not recorded. When I arrived, I saw the head of peeds and wanted to share the recording with her, but alas, could not."

HOW SHE WORKS

for Becky

On this floor, the fifth above earth,
she caroms from the desk to a girl

whose cast licks skin to steel, and
in her cartoon suit the cast becomes

a wand to whisk the elevator
to waiting family. Downstairs,

at lunch with her daughter, there is
a quarter hour for the flight of swings

before the comet of young lives,
torn from the hotel of absent parents, resumes.

She stops their eyes with a grin—the ruby
light of work begins: *I'm here—*

tell me your story. She has already given
this time to an unfinished labor

as if overcome with the dominion
of children, who slant in metal beds,

wait to hear the one right sound: *Go home.*
The fear is done. You are strong.

SEPTEMBER 23, 2003

"Today is the first day of autumn, and it is my last day in rounds. A sad day—I will miss the peeds staff, miss the camaraderie and the incredible searching that goes on. But I must finish the book and move on. I may drop in just because I have grown so close to the staff. One of the physical therapists had dinner with my young motorcycle friend—he's doing fine, prosthesis and all, even talking about getting back on the bike. Crazy, but the choice is his."

AUTUMNAL EQUINOX

This is the time of leaf fall.
In the red glow of southern sun,
there is a slow yearn to autumn.

It was a white season when I turned
to the cross of hands in cribs
and the hymns of mothers who sang *vive*.

Now is the time of letting leaves down
to the waiting cold. And like them,
I burnish with the journey to decay.

My innocence protected me
in this dormitory of healing.
Now I have come to the edge of fall—

the breaking of weather that builds
to final storm. It is the time of leaf fall,
the laying down of skin

and the wait for watery birth.
All day does life let go and end.
The ordinary death of leaves

is no less a symbol in this building:
spring may yet come to christen the child
who cannot pretend to leave

the orbit of hands in his lair.
This is the time of leaf fall—
when death drums first and last.

OCTOBER 7, 2003

"Came down to rounds to learn of Wilena's passing—the Scottish nurse whose ebullient presence in pediatrics cheered young hearts and minds for 11 years. I remember one Tuesday when she was in the hospital for a transfusion and came up to the fifth floor to cheer up a young motorcycle rider. She was funny, bright, and down to earth. She knew what kids wanted and gave it to them: abundant love and kindness. How she managed to laugh when so many were hurting was her particular gift. At noon I was giving a reading for the pediatric staff and wondered if, instead, we should just be silent. At last, I came back to read, to honor her erstwhile spirit in that room."

SONG FOR WILENA

You bubble into rounds
with cheekfuls of praise
for the children
who hide and wink—
the Scottish nurse
who shields them
from the pegs
of medicine.

For months
you sabered with cells
in the wild of your body
until one morning,
on the subject of diet,
you announced
to all low-carb sinners,
I have chained the fridge shut.

Wilena, namesake
of the island to poets
hungered by fog—
your face is rounder this day,
as if a child
aged in your midst.
We kiss you now
and leave the leaving to family.

STEPHEN DAVIS

Stories from the Front Lines

ARTIST'S STATEMENT

I spent the first three months of 2001 as artist-in-residence at Washoe Medical Center. I was honored to be one of three artists chosen to participate in this program. The three individuals most responsible for instituting the program—Jan Johnson of Washoe Medical Center, Steven High of the Nevada Museum of Art, and artist Jim McCormick—were very helpful throughout the program. Washoe Medical Center was especially supportive, giving me carte blanche to work in any department of the hospital.

At first this was somewhat overwhelming; the hospital was vast and it was hard to know where to start. Eventually I met three wonderful people who led the cancer support group. Sally DeLipkau, Kay MacDonald, and the Rev. Bob Fuller made me feel welcome and introduced me to the members of the group, people who were bravely struggling with their cancer. All participants were cooperative and allowed me to interview and photograph them.

Eventually, I was introduced to the staff of the Oncology unit. These front-line troops in the battle with cancer were also welcoming and cooperative. One staff member, Edythe Garvey, described what her work meant to her in a way that affected me greatly. Through these dedicated people I was introduced to patients, young and old, men and women, at different points in their struggle.

The goal of my work is, through images and text, to tell people's stories. When I find a topic of real interest to me, I want to know about other people's experiences on the same topic. This hospital residency was different because I was not sick and I did not have a medical story of my own to tell. However, I thought that the immediacy of this storytelling technique would draw attention to this all-too-common human experience.

My approach was to visit people in their homes or in their hospital rooms. I'd bring along a tape recorder and camera gear. I learned from my wife, a clinical psychologist, that the best approach is to ask open-ended questions and then keep quiet. Most people were willing to share intimate details about their struggle with cancer. I then listened to the tapes again and again until I found the story that seemed to summarize the person, their particular situation, and their approach to their illness. I learned about courage and the unique ways that people employ to cope with this life-threatening predicament. These strategies range from humor to fierce combativeness to a deepening of family ties. In "Steve's Story," for example, we come face to face with a former Marine who attacks his cancer as if he were assaulting the beach of an enemy atoll in World War II. Sally and Mary's stories show how humor can be a component in an intense determination to fight their disease. Since we are all just a telephone call or a doctor's visit away from finding ourselves in this same position, it would be wise to take note of these courageous individuals.

From time to time I have been asked whether I found this experience depressing. My answer is no. The adrenaline was certainly pumping when I walked into the hospital room of a stranger who had recently been given a cancer diagnosis. Some had a real need to talk, to tell their stories. Some were lonely and wanted to talk—about their childhoods, how they learned about their cancer, and about their plans for the future. Perhaps I was only seeing the face presented to the world, but to me these people were courageous and heroic. I felt like a young soldier preparing for combat who is surrounded by brave combat veterans. I couldn't help but think about how I would react in a similar situation, would I be strong or weak, what story would I tell. I really don't know. I thought of my own father's death from pancreatic

cancer, and I wished that I had known more about how he handled it.

I don't think that I can express the honor I felt at being permitted to spend time with these gutsy people. Oncology nurse Edythe Garvey best expressed my reaction to the time I spent with cancer patients when she said that "it's only a couple of tears. People always say it's so depressing, but it is moving and enlightening. You can't go through life without passion. You have to have something that you love—you have to feel things. You have to let things affect you."

STEPHEN DAVIS

STEVE'S STORY

I was a Marine in the Vietnam War and later a police officer and a court bailiff. What I learned in the Marines was duty, honor, and a sense of self-worth.

Last year I lost my voice. Eventually my doctor sent me to a specialist who discovered a tumor around my lung the size of a baseball. It scared the living hell out of me. I'm only 56 years old.

One surgeon told me that I had only a 20 – 30% chance; I said a few things under my breath about his parentage and I got a better doctor. I found a young fellow that I really like. He needed to shrink my tumor before he could operate so we did chemo and radiation. I've got so much chemistry in me now I feel like DuPont. I have so much radiation I feel like Yucca Flat.

My attitude is, "I've got cancer but I choose to manage it; it is not going to manage me."

When I was a Marine we were taught that we never leave our wounded behind and we never leave our dead behind. We never surrender. My family tradition is that we just don't quit. We've had our good times and we've had our bad times. But when you tell me that I'm going to die at 56 years old, you've just insulted me.

My attitude toward my cancer is the same as that of the commander of the Marines at Chosin Reservoir in Korea.

A regiment of Marines was cut off for seven days when they were surrounded by nine Chinese divisions. They were out of ammo, they were out of food, they had nothing. It was -50 degrees, and they only had tarpaulins to keep warm. The commander said, "Okay men, we've got 'em exactly where we want 'em." I rest my case. It isn't much of a war but it's the only one we've got. So let's scrap. I'm going to win this thing.

Here is what I'm going to do. First, I want to get rid of this cancer—surgery. The recovery period will take a month, maybe less. Then I'm going go to see my cousins in Germany. I need some good German beer and some good German food. It will probably do my stomach a world of good to get some real food in me. I want to go to the gym because I don't want to be oatmeal. And finally, I'd just like to be a decent human being. I'd like to be an advocate for those who don't have a voice.

I also want to get back to my Harley. I want to ride across Canada. I want to take the bike up to Vancouver. I'm going to stay at the Grand Hotel; I'm going to have high tea. I'm going to start off the next day, point due east and ride.

My advice to other people is don't be afraid, and don't ever, ever, ever quit.

RICHARD'S STORY

I was born in the little town of Georgetown, Idaho. After high school I fired locomotives for the Northern Pacific Railroad. That was a truly great job which I worked until World War II started. After the war I had a burnin' yearnin' for learnin' and so I went back to school. After college I worked in businesses of many kinds. I moved to Reno in 1962 and I retired in 1984.

When I retired my wife asked me what I was going to do, I told her I'd fouled up enough careers so I'm going to be a couch potato. She asked, "Why don't you go into politics." That's hard work. It's hard work getting elected, it's hard work serving. If you're honest the pay is lousy. I'm not smart enough to be crooked—I'd get caught. You're called dirty names. So, I said no. She said, "Would you mind if I went into politics?" I told her that if she had the fire in her belly to do it she should run for the Nevada Assembly—all the time I knew she didn't have a chance. Well, she just won her 8th term in the Nevada State Assembly. To some men this would be a fate worse than death. The politician's spouse is supposed to stand ten feet away with their hands folded with a big smile for everybody. This doesn't bother me at all.

She loves what she is doing and she does a good job. She is probably the best unknown in the Nevada State Assembly if not in all of politics. No one knows who Assemblywoman Vivian Freeman is, I swear, but she gets a great deal accomplished.

At Christmas time I buy six boxes of cherry chocolates at a time. I ate too many of them and I got a bellyache which lasted three days. By the time I saw my doctor my stomachache was gone. However, I mentioned that I'd lost twenty pounds in the year 2000. I hadn't even tried to lose it. He said, "That troubles me." He told me to go get some pictures taken. First ultrasound, then a CAT scan.

Here, let me show you my dirty picture. Look at the colors of these pictures. Look what they can come up with nowadays to scare you. You can see blood here, you can see blood around here. I had a biopsy on my colon. They really went in because the pictures showed that the liver was bad. They didn't know whether it was malignant until they went in to do a biopsy. They can fix the gut and the other things, but if the liver is bad that's a death . . . ah, the end, ah, that's the final enchilada. And, that is what it has turned out to be. My liver can't be repaired and that is a death sentence. There aren't too many of us who know when we are going to die.

I don't want radiation or chemotherapy. I've heard of people who've had it. I don't want to get well in order to die. So I'm not going to go that route.

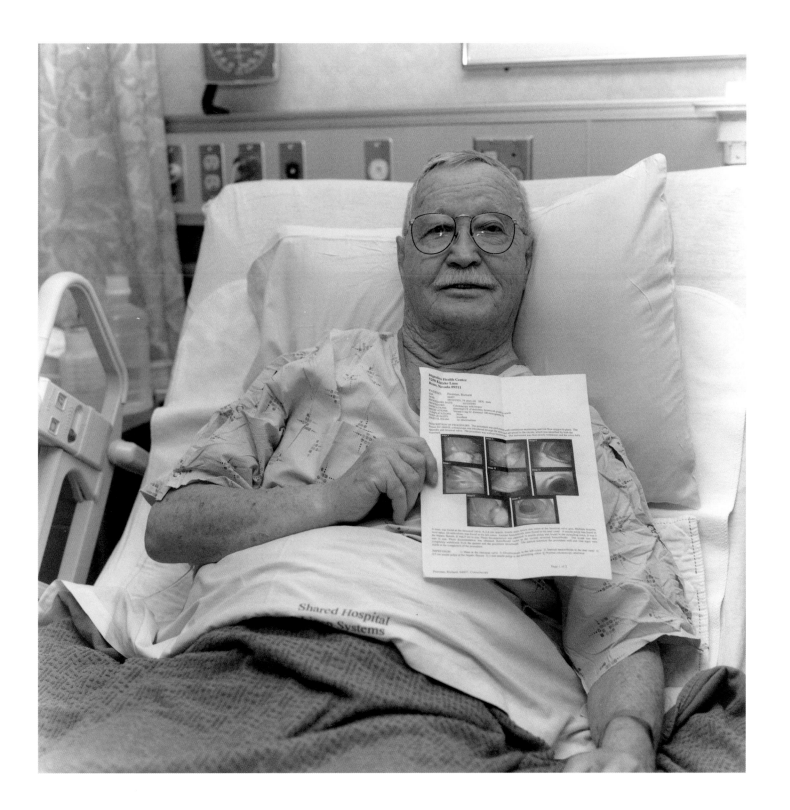

MARY'S STORY

I had surgery for ovarian cancer in June 2000. After my third chemotherapy I received a call from my surgeon who wanted me to join him for an interview on a local TV health program. I responded so well to treatment that he considered me a textbook case.

I got nervous as the interview grew near. The evening before, two of my daughters gave me a practice interview. Afterwards they assured me that I would do just fine. One daughter told me to settle down, "You're acting as though you're going to have a pelvic exam on TV." God forbid!

After briefly talking to me, the interviewer asked the doctor how he wished to proceed. He told her that I was due for a pelvic exam and would conduct the interview while he examined me. I was so nervous when he handed me a gown; it didn't cross my mind to refuse. The exam was done in good taste, but then it hit me: I wasn't wearing toenail polish. Can you believe it? I'm probably the only person in Reno to have a pelvic exam on TV, and my only concern was, "Oh my God, I didn't polish my toenails!"

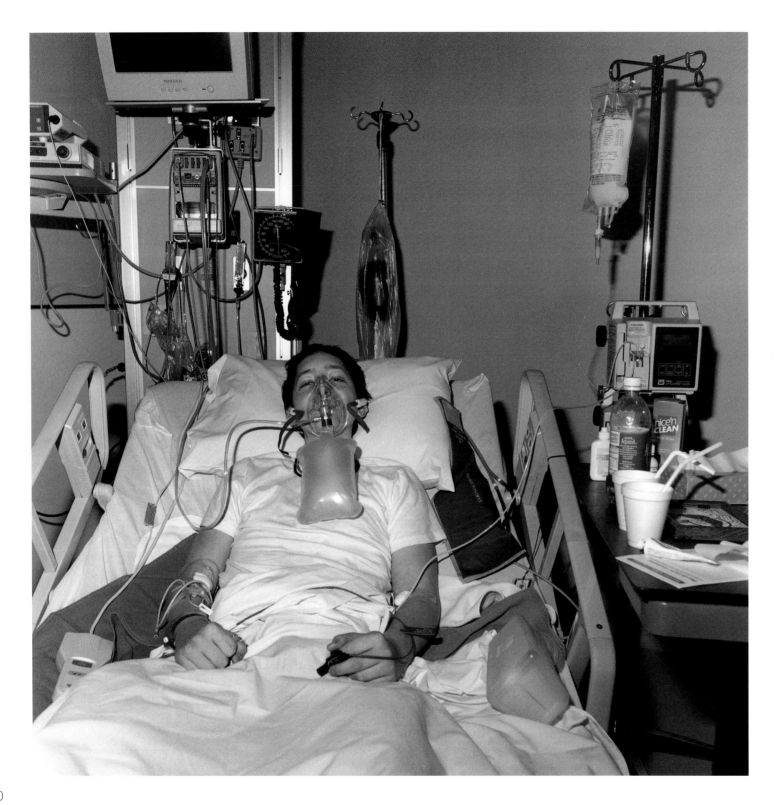

JOHN'S STORY

My name is John and I've been sick for over a year now. Before I got sick my favorite things were soccer and hockey, and playing my guitar. I like to play blues the most. B.B. King is my favorite—I also like Eric Clapton.

What I miss most is the easy stuff, the simple things. Like waking up and not having to worry—or, just going to school with my friends.

LAVONNE'S STORY

My name is Lavonne and I am a 37-year-old mother. I have four wonderful children and I'm soon to be a grandmother.

I was first diagnosed with ovarian cancer in 1998. Everyone kept telling me it was stress because I had a lot of marital problems. Other people were telling me that it was the change of life.

After treatment and a vacation I started a new job. I was feeling great until January of 2000. But soon I started feeling funny so I went to the doctor. I kept telling him that there was something wrong with my kidneys, I knew something was wrong. You just know—your body tells you something's not right. Well he didn't want to take my word for it. He kept giving me just pain pills, and he told me not to worry, my cancer couldn't come back—it was just the after-effects of radiation, etc., etc.   I collapsed in April of last year and was rushed to the Emergency Room.

Right now there is not a whole lot they can do. The tumor is wrapped around my bladder and my colon. The doctor can do an operation, but even with that the most they can give me is seven months. They will monitor my pain medication and I'm going to do the best I can 'til it's my time. It's hard; it's real hard.

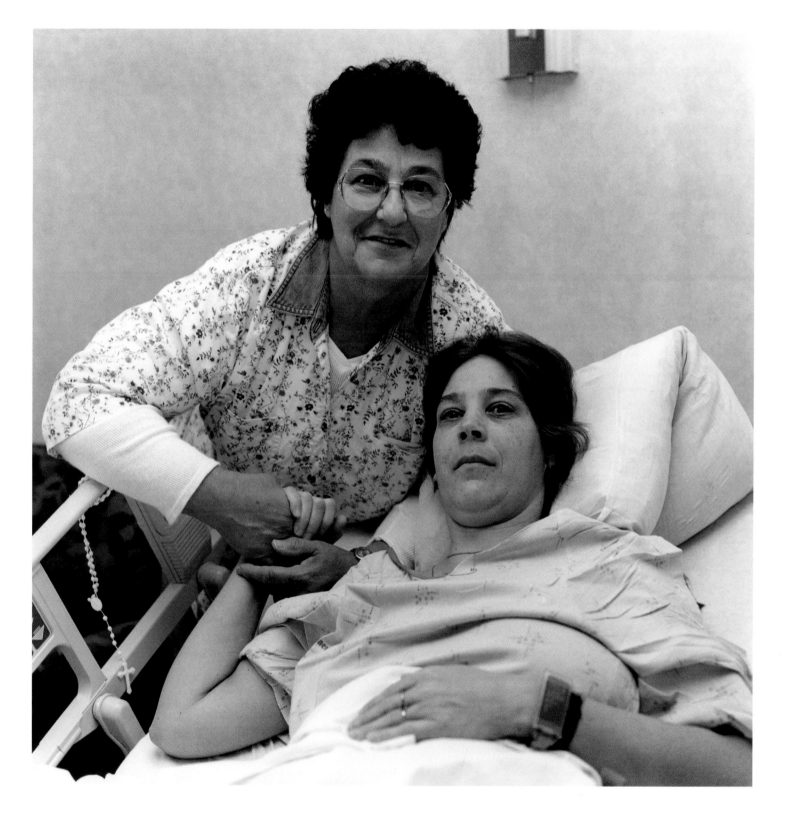

GAYNEL AND MAYA'S STORY

Gaynel: We met in '94 when we both worked for Reno Air. I'm a nut on full moons, so on the first full moon of our relationship, on a warm summer evening, we went on a picnic. After that we would drive to the top of the mountains for full moon picnics every chance we got. People thought we were nuts. One time we even got stuck in the snow on the top of Peavine.

Jeff: We got engaged at the top of Mount Rose under a full moon. When we got to the very top, I got down on my knees, pulled out a ring, and proposed. There were two guys camping up there. I asked them to take a picture. One guy looked at me and said, "Full moon, top of Mount Rose—you stud. You stud, give me that camera." They yelled the wedding march as we walked down to our campsite.

Gaynel: I didn't have energy for several months. It took the doctors six weeks to figure it out. They finally sent me to a gastro specialist. He was the one who found it. That's why I'm a really strong advocate of colonoscopy. The mass was the size of a hard ball—it was almost a 100% blockage.

Jeff: Gaynel being Gaynel, never takes anything at face value, never anything. She must do her own research. She's like a pit bull; she won't stop. She had to learn everything.

Jeff: Three days after Christmas our grandbaby Maya, who was 19 months old, was diagnosed with kidney cancer and we were back on the roller coaster. It was a nightmare on top of a nightmare. Your prayers are always to protect your children.

Gaynel: To see your child go through the pain of having a child with cancer was more heart-wrenching than my own illness. Maya had surgery in Oakland and then came home for chemo. I knew what it felt like, so I held her in my arms the very first time she got chemo. She looked up at me and she gasped and said, "Grandma, it's cold." She could feel it going in through the tube in her chest.

Jeff: Maya has maturity beyond her years. The first time she saw Gaynel get her daily shot she came running in, jumped up on the bed, and grabbed Grandma's hand and held it. She said, "It's okay, Grandma, it's okay." She is very aware and has tremendous sensitivity.

Gaynel: The American Cancer Society has a Race for the Cure every year. The first lap is the survivors' lap and I was determined to do that with Maya because we are going to be survivors, no matter what. It took me all day to get out of bed but we did the first lap together.

NANCY'S STORY

I worked at Washoe as a registered nurse for 31 years. I discovered that I had cancer when I had a sudden onset of back pain that got steadily worse. After two months it was really severe. I'm feeling better now that they have the pain and nausea under control.

I have multiple myeloma, which is a fast-growing bone cancer. What happens is some little cells in the plasma go berserk. They begin to munch away on the bone and then what they do is they dump their byproducts into your blood stream so, all of a sudden, you have very high calcium and lots of other weird proteins in your blood. That's one of the tip-offs—strange blood studies.

I taught for a long while in nursing education. I also worked seventeen years in emergency rooms at night. When I was at Washoe we didn't have a cancer ward. When I came here the only differentiation was between medical and surgical and men and women. We didn't have special wards—we didn't even have an ICU.

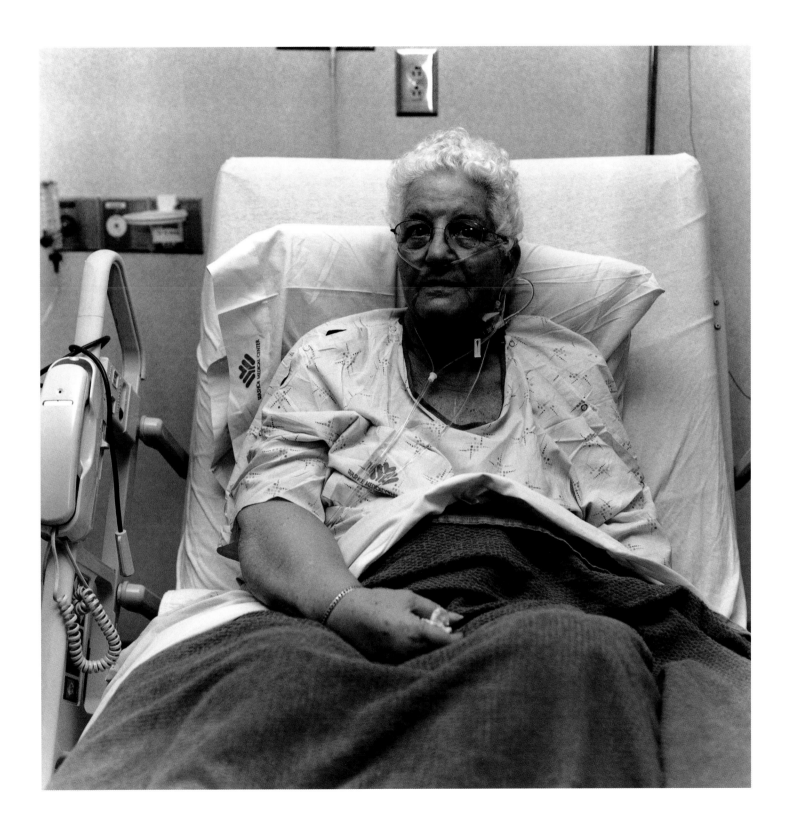

EDYTHE'S STORY
clinical nurse specialist for oncology

I can get people to finish their final work, to put things in perspective, to figure out life. You really have to have your head on right as far as what life's about and what you want. I'm very clear about what I want and what I don't want in life.

A lot of times I talk to people about what they feel they need to get done before life is over. Sometimes it's giving away things, writing letters, apologizing, and leaving a legacy for their children.

I don't know. I love doing it. It gives you a rich life. It's only a couple of tears. People always say it's so depressing, but it is moving and enlightening. You can't go through life without passion. You have to have something that you love—you have to feel things. You have to let things affect you.

SALLY'S STORY
patient representative

My husband left in February of '79, my father died in March, and I was diagnosed with breast cancer in November—it was quite a year. The pain and the trauma and the hurt, that bone-deep pain from my husband leaving, really prepared me for cancer. I went home to tell my children. I told my boy, "Something's wrong with mom's boob and they are going to have to take it off." He said, "And then they'll fix it and put it back on?"

In 1986, after remarrying, I started to feel crummy. I really couldn't put my finger on it. I had pains, I didn't have a lot of energy, and I was short of breath. After a complete physical showed nothing, the doctor suggested that maybe a little therapy might be in order.

After another blood test, my doctor called immediately and said, "I think you have cancer." I asked him how the two blood tests could have been so different. He said, "Well, your counts on the first one were so bad I thought they had made a mistake. I didn't think you could be walking around with blood like that."

I was referred to an oncologist who discovered that the cancer had eaten up my bone marrow. While I was getting dressed I could hear him chewing out my doctor over the phone. He said, "I can't believe, with her history . . . She's almost dead." My husband is a lawyer and all doctors cringe when they have a lawyer's wife as a patient!

I always tell people, "Boy, you have to have that relationship with the guy or gal who's saving your life." You have to be comfortable with them and trust them. I absolutely trusted him and the treatment. You have to use every tool available.

I felt as though my body had turned on me—what did I do wrong? Is it a God thing—have I not been a good person? You wonder if this is your punishment. I think we all do that because we want to know a reason so we can change that. I did a lot of reading, which helped. Some of my favorites are the old classics like *Anatomy of an Illness* and *When Bad Things Happen to Good People* by Rabbi Kushner. His philosophy is that God makes us human and with that comes all the human stuff. No one is chosen to have the bad things happen. I got a lot of comfort out of that. I think having had cancer made me more patient and tolerant than I was before. I always cared about people but I cared about them in a different way, because I've been exactly where they are. No matter where that is, I've been there.

ARTIST BIOGRAPHIES

STEPHEN DAVIS

Stephen Davis is a documentary photographer whose work investigates his dual interests in the humanities and photography. His work includes studies of agricultural land use in Minnesota, California, and Nevada; a survey of open lands remaining in the Truckee Meadows, and a documentary on the early phases of the Double Diamond Ranch development in Reno, Nevada.

Over the last fifteen years he has concentrated on projects that tell stories through text and photographs. An example is a body of work on childhood memory and sense of place in the Truckee Meadows.

Davis holds a Ph.D. in American history from the University of Wisconsin, Madison. He is Assistant Director at Nevada Humanities, where he oversees cultural programs statewide.

His work has been exhibited at the Art Institute of Chicago, the Sheppard Gallery at the University of Nevada, Reno, and the Nevada State Legislature Gallery in Carson City.

Davis lives in Reno with his wife and two children.

SHAUN T. GRIFFIN

Shaun Griffin is the co-founder and director of Community Chest, a non-profit agency serving children and families in northwestern Nevada since 1991, and the founder and former director of the state's homeless education office. Shaun has spent a lifetime trying to build bridges where there were none for all members of the human community. During the mid-80s he worked in Stanford University's foremost community outreach program, starting several disability initiatives on that campus. He later founded a minority youth outreach program for four universities in the San Francisco Bay Area. In 2004, he received the Mike O'Callaghan Humanitarian Award, named after the former Nevada governor.

His last book of poems was *Bathing in the River of Ashes*, published by the University of Nevada Press in 1999. *Death to Silence* (translations from the Chilean poet Emma Sepúlveda) was released by Arte Público Press in 1997. In 1995 he received the Governor's Award for Excellence in the Arts.

For many years he has taught a poetry workshop at Northern Nevada Correctional Center and published an annual journal of prisoners' work, *Razor Wire*. He regularly contributes poetry, essays, and translations to literary journals in the West, and was editor-at-large of *Calapooya* and contributing editor of *Weber Studies*. He is trying to finish a memoir about a long journey with his family from Tokyo to Patagonia—*The House of a Thousand Arms*.

He has lived in Nevada since 1978—except for the four years when his wife was in graduate school in the Bay Area. He and his family live in Virginia City, at the western-most edge of the Great Basin.

SHARON MACZKO

Born in Michigan in 1958, Sharon Maczko is a self-taught artist, working primarily in transparent watercolors, her medium of choice for over 30 years. With a roster of seven solo exhibitions as well as an extensive number of group exhibitions, she has also written for and/or had her artwork published in several magazines and eight books, including a textbook for grade schoolers titled *Art Express*; the "Splash" series of watercolor books from North Light Press; and recently, an instructional watercolor book published in London, England.

Maczko has won numerous awards for her artwork, including four grants collectively from the Nevada Arts Council and Sierra Arts Foundation. Her work is included in many private and corporate collections, including the San Diego Museum of Art. Although she established her art career in California, she currently produces work from her studio in Wellington, Nevada. Maczko's artwork is represented by Stremmel Gallery in Reno, Nevada.

With all of her accomplishments, she feels the Artist In Residence program at Washoe Medical Center was her most important achievement.

All artist photos by Steve Young, Medical Photographer for Washoe Medical Center.

POEMS

PAINTINGS

PHOTOGRAPHS

SPECIAL THANKS

Many years ago I had in my life a wonderful and strong teenager who despite her critical illness managed to be the impetus for several poems. Many of those poems were put to music and shared with patients at the Mayo Clinic in Rochester, Minnesota.

The musical healing that was generated was both inspiring to others and an awesome credit to those who were touched by her life. Most especially Theresa and Don Stewart. An elevator operator who came to know the teenager wrote the poems, and the music was composed and recorded by a musician who worked at the clinic. That experience inspired me to try to keep art in healing at the forefront of my career. The teenager died, but the art in healing lives on through such artists as those whose work is shared in this collection.

It has been an inspiration for me to know these artisans and have the joy of the friendship that has developed with each of them. Each of the artists, Sharon, Stephen, and Shaun, as well as Steven High, Jim McCormick, and the staff of Washoe Medical Center have worked in concert to bring the publication of this collection to reality.

Partial funding for this program was through the foresight of Rollan Melton and the John Ben Snow Foundation.

Jan Johnson, Director, Washoe Medical Foundation